Great Greeks

Written by Paul Perro

Illustrated by D.McRae

Contents

Introduction

Perhaps you think your granddad's old?
Perhaps you've got antiques?
But those aren't really old at all
Compared to Ancient Greeks.
They lived thousands of years ago
Way back in ancient times.
Let's learn about them now shall we?
Here come some little rhymes.

The City States

The Ancient Greek cities
Were all quite separate.
Athens, Thebes, and Sparta -
Each one a different state.
These city states sometimes
Decided to unite,
Usually when enemies
Came to pick a fight.

Alexander the Great

The best ever military commander
Was a young king named Alexander.
From the Macadonian city state,
He was known as Alexander the Great.
A brave man - he had a lot of bottle;
A wise man too - taught by Aristotle.
He fought many battles and always won,
His army never lost a single one.
Turkey, Syria and Egypt all fell,
So did Babylon, and Persia as well.
But after 13 years of war, his men
Said they wanted to go home again.
That was the end of conquest and glory
And that's the end of Alexander's story

Those Clever Greeks

The Ancient Greeks invented many things,
Like water mills, steam engines, and maps.
They founded democracy,
Drama and philosophy,
The Ancient Greeks were really clever chaps.

Astronomers

Astronomers from Greece worked out
The Earth goes round the sun.
It took hundreds of years before
Everyone else caught on.

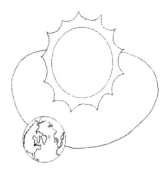

Mathematicians

The genius Archimedes once had
An idea that made him shout "Eureka"
He jumped out his bath, and ran down the path,
Then ran about naked like a streaker!
Another genius called Pythagoras
Once discovered a very famous sum.
This guy though, unlike the other fellow,
Did not show everyone his bum.

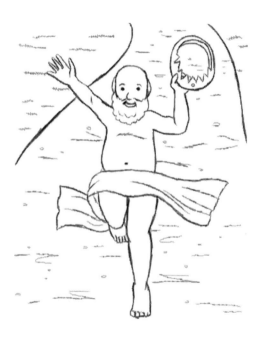

Philosophers

Philosophers were thinkers, wise men,

And most of the greats were Greeks.

Like Aristotle, Socrates,

Plato and Diogenes.

If they lived today we'd call them "geeks".

Doctors

Hippocrates, the doctor,
Laid medicine's foundation.
He pioneered a technique called
Clinical observation.
This means he used proven facts
Not silly superstitions.
He is still revered today
By doctors and physicians.

Historians

If Herodotus
Had not invented history,
Events of the past would have
Always remained a mystery.

Democracy

Athens was the birthplace
Of democracy.
They had a vote to choose
Who their leader would be.

Pericles was the most
Popular bar none.
He was elected 15 times.
He built the Parthenon.

The Seven Wonders of the World

Do they walk on their heads
In the place they call "Down Under"?
This is something about which
I often stop and wonder.

The seven wonders of the world
Are a different sort of thing.
They're things you wonder <u>at</u>
Because they're so amazing.

The Greeks chose seven buildings
Which were splendid and unique,
And purely by coincidence
Most of them were Greek.

The Colossus of Rhodes

The people of the island Rhodes
Once built a huge metal statue.
A bit like that one in New York,
Except it was not greeny blue.

They made it from bronze which they took
From the armour of an enemy.
When the sun glistened on it it was
A glorious sight to see.

The Hanging Basket of Babylon

The hanging basket of Babylon
Was...oops I do beg your pardons,
Did I say hanging basket?
I meant to say hanging gardens.

Built by Nebuchadnezzar,
A gift for his homesick queen;
To remind her of her homeland,
A mountainous land, lush and green.

The Statue of Zeus at Olympia

A statue of the mighty Zeus;
Of all the gods, he was the king.
The columns were in the "Doric" style,
If you care about that sort of thing.

Built to honour the Olympic Games,
The statue is now long gone,
But the stadium has been rebuilt
And the spirit of the games lives on.

The Mausoleum of Halicarnassus

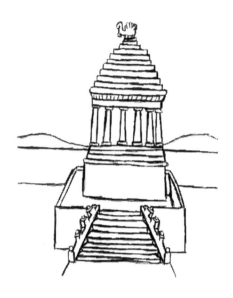

Built by Queen Artemisia,
A tomb for her husband, the king,
The mausoleum was said to be
A very beautiful building.

Yes, the tomb of King Mausolus
Was certainly ostentatious.
And also, for just one person
It was really very spacious.

The Lighthouse at Alexandria

On the cliffs of the island of Pharos,
A lighthouse guided ships into port.
People went there especially to see it,
It became a tourist resort.

Eventually an earthquake destroyed it
And it fell in the sea, and sank.
A visiting tourist today would need
A wet suit and an oxygen tank.

The Temple at Ephesus

Someone once burned this temple down,
A man who just wanted some fame.
The Ephesians punished him by banning
Everyone from saying his name.

The temple was destroyed a few times
But each time they built it back grander.
Everyone agreed it was beautiful,
Even the great Alexander.

The Great Pyramid at Giza

The Ancient Egyptians built
The great pyramid.
Did they really?
Yes they really did.

'Twas once the tallest building ever,
Taller than the treetops.
It was built as a tomb for
An Egyptian pharaoh called Cheops.

Homer

Homer (that's the poet from Greece,
Not the fat bald man from TV)
Wrote the poem called "The Iliad",
He also wrote "The Odyssey".

The Iliad

The Iliad tells the story,
Set during the long Trojan War
Of the Greek hero Achilles,
And his triumph over Hector.

The Odyssey

The story of Odysseus
Is told in Homer's "Odyssey" -
His epic quest to get back home
To see his wife Penelope.
He had some bother on the way
With women with hypnotic powers,
A cyclops, a witch, a monster,
And folk who liked to eat flowers.

The History of the Olympics

I guess you know the Olympic Games,
You've heard about them, probably.
But did you know they first began
In 776 BC.

'Twas Hercules who founded them
So he could celebrate
His most recent heroic act;
'Twas something really great.
He'd cleaned a filthy stable that
Was full of horse manure.
...Well, that's the legend anyway,
Nobody knows for sure.

There were lots of sports and games:
Running, throwing, jumping,
And something called "pankration" -
Wrestling, with thumping.

Back then all athletes competed
Completely in the nude.
If somebody did that today
We'd think it very rude.

One day a Christian Emperor
Named Theodosius
Stopped the games completely,
Because they honoured Zeus.

But hundreds of years later, at
The end of Queen Vic's reign,
Somebody had the bright idea
To bring them back again.

<u>Mythical Creatures</u>

The ancient Greeks believed in
Some really crazy things,
Like minotaurs, centaurs,
And a horse with wings.

The Gods

The Greeks believed in many gods,
A few dozen, or so.
They lived on Mount Olympus and
Watched mortal men below.

Mighty Zeus was the king,
Poseidon ruled the sea,
Hades ruled the underworld -
These were the ruling three.

That's all I have to say for now.
This is the end; we're through.
I hope you have enjoyed these poems
And learned a thing or two.

THE END

Made in the USA
Lexington, KY
16 January 2015